Pocket Personality Quiz

Series Editor: Heather Dickson
Written and researched by: Deirdre MacDonald
Additional contributors: Catherine Gordon
Illustrations: Gaby Wirminghaus
Page design and layout: Linley Clode
Cover design: Gary Inwood Studios

Published by:
LAGOON BOOKS
PO BOX 311, KT2 5QW, UK

ISBN: 1899712909

LAGOON BOOKS, 1999

Printed in Singapore

Pocket Personality Quiz

LAGOON
BOOKS

Other titles available from Lagoon Books:

Where in the World Am I?
ISBN 1899712410

Pub Trivia Quiz
ISBN 189971250X

Who in the World Am I?
ISBN 1899712275

Sports Trivia Quiz
ISBN 1899712267

Sporting Record-Breakers
ISBN 1899712755

The Ultimate Football Quiz
ISBN 1899712747

The Ultimate Golf Quiz
ISBN 1899712739

All books can be ordered from bookshops by
quoting the above ISBN numbers.

Introduction

At last! The opportunity to discover
your true characteristics!

How do you see yourself? Is it the same way that you think
other people perceive you? Are you ambitious?
Are you an extrovert? Do you know whether you have any
creative genes in your body or whether you have a purely
logical and organised mind? Are you laid-back or are you
fast-paced, impatient and stressed? Do you see the world
through rose-tinted glasses or do you paint everything in
black and white?

You gave that special someone a Valentine last February,
but does that make you a true romantic? Do you wear
your heart on your sleeve and plan intimate candle-lit
celebrations for two or is your idea of a dream date a
TV dinner and the latest omnibus edition of your favourite
soap? Turn to Chapter 2 and test yourself to see.
Better still, take turns to answer the questions with your
partner to find out their idea of a dream date, whether
they believe in love at first sight and what puts them in
the mood!

Alternatively, find out more about your personality from
your choice of colours (Chapter 8), the size and shape of
your head (Chapter 4) and the angle of your handwriting
(Chapter 10).

Find out something different about your personality in
every chapter.

INDEX

CHAPTER ONE

STRIVING AND STRESSED OR
LOW-KEY AND LAID BACK?

Are you assertive, fast-paced
and impatient or calm, easy-going
and quiet. Take your pulse with
this questionnaire and find out.
Simply consider each pair of statements
and circle the number closest to the
statement you feel applies most to you.

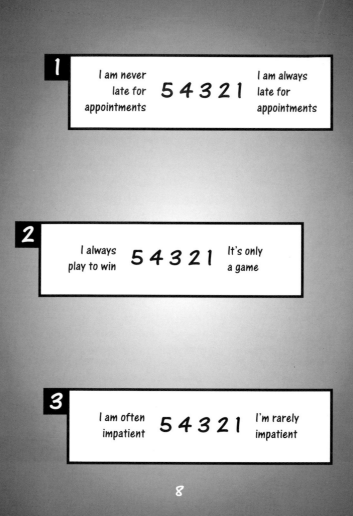

1

I am never late for appointments   5 4 3 2 1   I am always late for appointments

2

I always play to win   5 4 3 2 1   It's only a game

3

I am often impatient   5 4 3 2 1   I'm rarely impatient

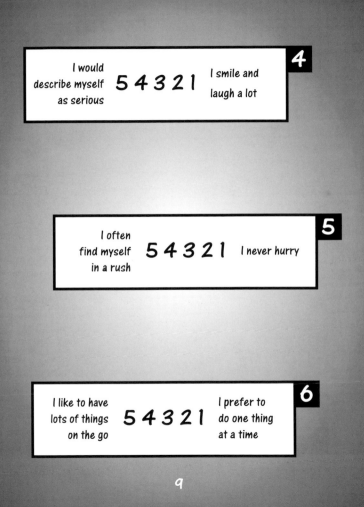

4

I would describe myself as serious 　5 4 3 2 1　 I smile and laugh a lot

5

I often find myself in a rush 　5 4 3 2 1　 I never hurry

6

I like to have lots of things on the go 　5 4 3 2 1　 I prefer to do one thing at a time

7

It's important to me that people notice if I've done something well

5 4 3 2 1

I do things for my own satisfaction

8

When I talk, I get quite animated and gesticulate a lot

5 4 3 2 1

I think before I speak and talk quietly and deliberately

9

I dislike talking about my feelings

5 4 3 2 1

I am very open and will talk about anything

10

Success and recognition are very important to me

5 4 3 2 1

I've never been career-orientated

11

I'm more of a talker than a listener

5 4 3 2 1

I'm a good listener

12

I like to be in control

5 4 3 2 1

I go with the flow

13

I push myself and others hard

5 4 3 2 1

I'm easy-going and relaxed

14

I hate queues, traffic jams and delays of any kind

5 4 3 2 1

Waiting is not a problem for me

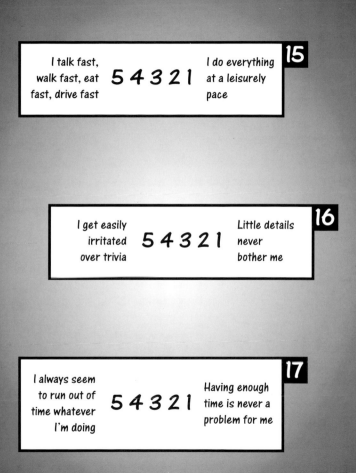

15

I talk fast, walk fast, eat fast, drive fast

5 4 3 2 1

I do everything at a leisurely pace

16

I get easily irritated over trivia

5 4 3 2 1

Little details never bother me

17

I always seem to run out of time whatever I'm doing

5 4 3 2 1

Having enough time is never a problem for me

18

I have no time for out-of-work activities   5 4 3 2 1   I have a lot of outside interests and hobbies

19

I get furious if I make a mistake   5 4 3 2 1   I never get angry with myself

20

I can be critical of others   5 4 3 2 1   I never find fault with others

NOW TURN TO PAGE 83

CHAPTER TWO

SOFT-CENTRE OR HARD NUT?

Romantic or just pragmatic? Are you the
type to get that practical little potato
peeler for the Christmas stocking or are
you the sort that buys the stocking?
Some types can't help wearing their
hearts on their sleeve or acting on impulse,
others wouldn't recognise Cupid if they
ran him over with a two-ton truck.
So, are you a fool for love?
Test yourself and see!

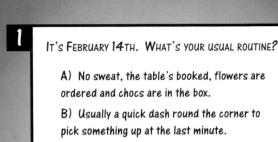

1 IT'S FEBRUARY 14TH. WHAT'S YOUR USUAL ROUTINE?

A) No sweat, the table's booked, flowers are ordered and chocs are in the box.

B) Usually a quick dash round the corner to pick something up at the last minute.

C) What's so special about February 14th?

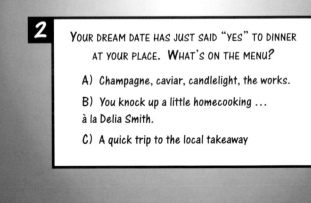

2 YOUR DREAM DATE HAS JUST SAID "YES" TO DINNER AT YOUR PLACE. WHAT'S ON THE MENU?

A) Champagne, caviar, candlelight, the works.

B) You knock up a little homecooking ...
à la Delia Smith.

C) A quick trip to the local takeaway

You've been offered a single ticket for that "once in a lifetime" event, but realise it clashes with that "secret" celebration your partner has been planning. Do you...?

A) Pass on the offer. After all, if you can't share the experience with your lover, it wouldn't be so good.

B) Initiate a pre-emptive strike by hinting heavily how tied up you are that day, forcing them to "secretly" rearrange all their plans.

C) Say nothing and go to the event. I mean, how were you to know they had been so foolish as to plan something without telling you!

4 HOW OFTEN DO YOU SURPRISE YOUR PARTNER WITH PRESENTS OR GESTURES OF AFFECTION?

A) All the time.

B) Once in a while.

C) You mean Birthdays and Christmas aren't enough?

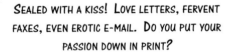

5 SEALED WITH A KISS! LOVE LETTERS, FERVENT FAXES, EVEN EROTIC E-MAIL. DO YOU PUT YOUR PASSION DOWN IN PRINT?

A) You just love to pen that purple prose.

B) You have been known to send the odd missive.

C) Only the occasional writ.

6

WHAT'S YOUR IDEA OF A GREAT NIGHT IN?

A) Intimate supper for two, a roaring fire and a full bottle of baby oil.

B) Good friends, good music and good wine.

C) A TV supper and the latest omnibus edition of your favourite soap/sport special.

7

IF MUSIC BE THE FOOD OF LOVE, WHAT PUTS YOU IN THE MOOD?

A) Emotional arias from the great operas.

B) A slow smoochy number.

C) Military band music.

8

DO YOU THINK THERE'S SOMEONE FOR
EVERYONE, A PERFECT MATE OUT THERE
SOMEWHERE WAITING TO BE FOUND?

A) Of course, it's what it's all about.

B) You'd like to think so...

C) Only a sucker would swallow that line!

9

YOUR LOVER/PARTNER LOOKS TIRED. WOULD YOU..?

A) Run a relaxing bath with aromatic oils,
surrounded by soothing scented candles.

B) Offer a massage and serve up a special meal.

C) Hand them a cup of tea, once they've finished
the washing up.

10

DO YOU BELIEVE IN "LOVE AT FIRST SIGHT",
THE "BOLT FROM THE BLUE"?

A) Definitely.

B) Lust maybe, but love ... mmm?

C) Only in films.

11

"LOVE IS BLIND" OR DO THOSE LITTLE FOIBLES OR
PERNICKETY PERSONAL HABITS GET YOU DOWN?

A) Such mannerisms are endearing, all part
of the charm.
B) Quid pro quo – you use their hair clippers to
trim your toe nails in the bath.
C) If you've told them once to stop doing that,
you've told them a hundred times!

12

YOU ARE PLANNING A TRIP ABROAD WITH
YOUR PARTNER. IT INVOLVES...

A) Watching spectacular sunsets and taking
moonlit strolls along exotic sandy beaches.
B) Trekking across the Indian subcontinent.
C) The West Face of the Eiger with crampons
and ice-picks.

13

IS A GOOD RELATIONSHIP FAIRLY SELF-SUFFICIENT OR DOES IT NEED LOTS OF CARE AND ATTENTION?

A) Love conquers all if left to its own devices.

B) Relationships take time and effort.

C) A detailed campaign strategy is required if either of you is to survive the encounter.

14

MAKING SPACE FOR QUALITY TIME TOGETHER FROM THE DEMANDS OF A BUSY SCHEDULE IS...

A) Never a problem.

B) More difficult than you would like.

C) A question of checking your diary for the next allocated R&R slot.

NOW TURN TO PAGE 84

CHAPTER THREE

ANIMAL MAGNETISM

Whether you love them or loathe them,
certain animals have come to be
associated with particular qualities
or characteristics. So, do you like
yours cute and cuddly, running
swift and free or just safe behind bars?

For this exercise, choose three animals,
from the pages overleaf, in order of
preference. Then turn to page 26.

NOW, FROM THE LISTS BELOW, SELECT FOUR
QUALITIES YOU ASSOCIATE WITH, ADMIRE IN, OR EVEN
DISLIKE ABOUT, THE ANIMALS YOU HAVE CHOSEN.

A	B	C	D
Bad-temper	Strength	Patience	Elusiveness
Cruelty	Courage	Fidelity	Rarity
Cunning	Nobleness	Docility	Solitariness
Predatory	Pride	Intelligence	Timidity
Ferocity	Wisdom	Playfulness	Cuteness
Swiftness	Agility	Curiosity	Stupidity
Obstinacy	Fecundity	Endurance	Laziness

Animal One

....
....
....
....

Animal Two

....
....
....
....

Animal Three

....
....
....
....

NOW TURN TO PAGE 85

CHAPTER FOUR

PHYSIOGNOMY – LET'S GET PHYSICAL

Can you be read like an open book or are you poker-faced? We all know about body language and the signals we give off, consciously or unconsciously, but what does our actual physical shape reveal about us? Have you got sensitive hands, an intelligent brow or a determined chin?

Let's take a look in the mirror and we'll see...

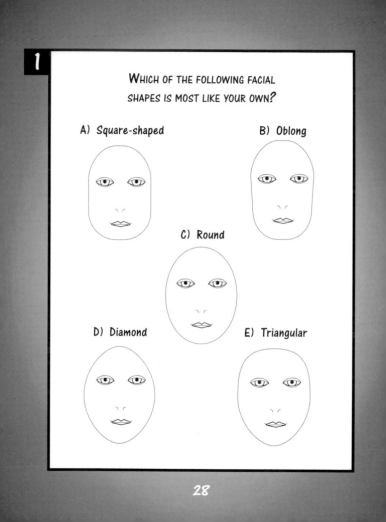

IF THE EYES ARE THE MIRRORS OF THE SOUL, WHAT ARE YOURS REFLECTING AND WHAT SHAPE ARE THEY?

A) Large

B) Small

C) Protruding

D) Deep set

E) Round

F) Almond-shaped

AND WHAT COLOUR ARE THEY?

A) Very dark brown, nearly black

B) Blue

C) Hazel

D) Grey

E) Green

WHETHER YOU PLUCK THEM, SMOOTH THEM, OR BRUSH THEM, YOUR EYEBROWS HAVE A NATURAL SHAPE IF LEFT TO THEIR OWN DEVICES. WHICH WOULD IT BE?

A) Long eyebrows

B) Short eyebrows

C) Normal eyebrows

D) Thin, delicate eyebrows

E) Bushy eyebrows

F) Joined eyebrows

G) Angular eyebrows

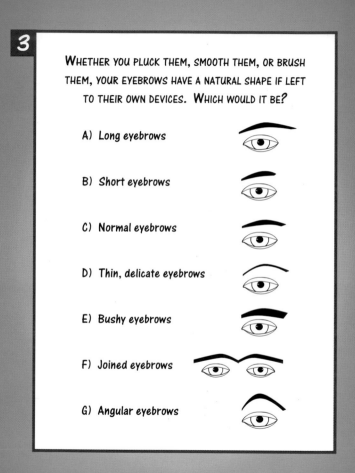

TIME TO INSPECT YOUR HANDS.
ARE THEY...

A) Square palm with short fingers

B) Rectangular palm with long fingers

C) Rectangular palm with short fingers

D) Square palm with long fingers

FINGER-LICKING GOOD OR JUST FUMBLING?
DIAGNOSE THOSE DIGITS.
WHAT SHAPE ARE YOUR FINGERS?

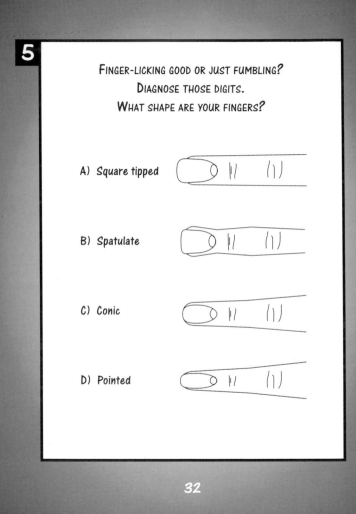

A) Square tipped

B) Spatulate

C) Conic

D) Pointed

LOOK AT THE THREE PHALANGES OF YOUR FINGERS. DOES ONE PART TEND TO BE LONGER THAN THE OTHERS?

A) Top joint
B) Middle phalange
C) Bottom section
D) Evenly balanced

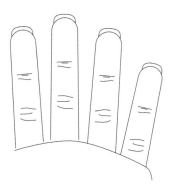

7

NOW FOR THE THUMB. USUALLY, THE TOP OF
THE THUMB CAN REACH THE BOTTOM PHALANGE
OF THE INDEX FINGER. IS YOURS...?

A) Normal

B) Short

C) Long

WHILE LOOKING AT THE THUMB, NOTE IF IT IS...

A) Low-set – can be positioned
at 90° angle to index finger

B) High-set – close to the hand

8

THE PHALANGES OF THE THUMB. ARE YOURS...?

A) Evenly balanced

B) Top longer/stronger

C) Second section longer/stronger

D) Bottom section prominent

9

10 IS YOUR THUMB WAISTED?

    A) Yes

    B) No

11 IS YOUR THUMB SUPPLE?

    A) No

    B) Slightly

    C) Very

ARE YOUR FINGERS IN PROPORTION TO EACH OTHER
OR DOES ONE DOMINATE? CHECK OUT THESE
MEASUREMENTS, THEN CHECK YOUR HAND.

INDEX FINGER: should be same length as ring finger –
slightly higher than half-way up the top phalange of the
middle finger.

MIDDLE FINGER: slightly less than half of the top phalange
should reach above the index and ring fingers.

RING FINGER: should be same length as the index finger –
slightly higher than half-way up the top phalange of the
middle finger.

LITTLE FINGER: should reach the top phalange of the ring
finger, but, if set low on the palm, will look shorter than it
actually is. In which case, place the little finger of one hand
over the ring finger of the other.

ARE ANY OF YOUR FINGERS
SIGNIFICANTLY OUT OF PROPORTION?

A) Index
B) Middle
C) Ring
D) Little

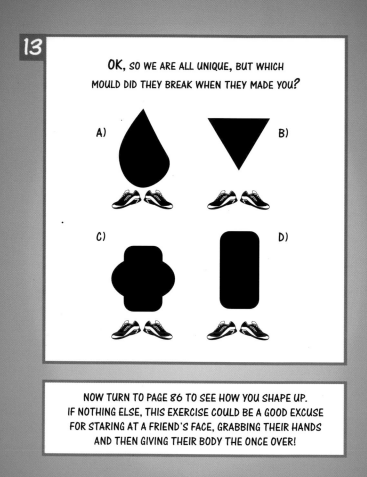

NOW TURN TO PAGE 86 TO SEE HOW YOU SHAPE UP.
IF NOTHING ELSE, THIS EXERCISE COULD BE A GOOD EXCUSE
FOR STARING AT A FRIEND'S FACE, GRABBING THEIR HANDS
AND THEN GIVING THEIR BODY THE ONCE OVER!

CHAPTER FIVE

A CARING LOVER OR CALLOUS CASANOVA?

Some types have real problems
when it comes to the
C words – Consideration,
Caring, Commitment.
Are you a lecherous louse,
loyal lover or just a wet blanket?
To find out, answer true or false
to each of the following questions...

1 It's the "physical chemistry" that first attracts you to someone. **T/F**

2 You enjoy the excitement of the chase, but quickly get bored once you've scored. **T/F**

3 You like to keep your lover on their toes and guessing. **T/F**

4 Good sex is always the driving factor in a relationship, while friendship and intellectual compatibility take a back seat. **T/F**

5 The cat's away and the mouse wants a quick nibble of a new piece of cheese – nobody would ever know. You would be tempted. **T/F**

6 Saying I love you is a means to an end. **T/F**

7 You think too much kissing and cuddling is for wimps. **T/F**

8 HAVING A QUICK BONK DOESN'T MEAN YOU HAVE TO GO ALL EMOTIONAL AND BECOME BOSOM BUDDIES OR ANYTHING. **T/F**

9 YOU AVOID EMOTIONAL INTIMACY TO AVOID GETTING INVOLVED, TO AVOID GETTING HURT. **T/F**

 10 YOU TEND TO GET THE HOTS MOST AND MAKE THE FIRST PASS. **T/F**

11 YOU'D RATHER GO OUT TO THE PUB WITH YOUR PALS THAN MAKE THE EFFORT TO MIX WITH YOUR LOVER'S FAMILY AND FRIENDS. **T/F**

 12 A FRIEND YOU HAVE ALWAYS SECRETLY FANCIED IS ON THE REBOUND AND NEEDS A FRIENDLY SHOULDER TO CRY ON. WHILE QUIETLY COMFORTING THEM, YOU ARE DESPERATELY PLANNING WHEN TO POUNCE. **T/F**

13 YOU FEEL COMFORTABLE TELLING YOUR PARTNER ABOUT WHAT YOU FIND SEXUALLY AROUSING. **T/F**

14 WHEN IT COMES TO SEXUAL SATISFACTION AND ACHIEVING THE BIG O, IT'S EVERYONE FOR THEMSELF AND FIRST PAST THE BEDPOST. **T/F**

15 THE LITTLE SPORTS CAR IS YOURS FOR THE TAKING, AS LONG AS YOU SLEEP WITH YOUR BOSS. YOU'D THINK WHY NOT? HE/SHE'S NOT THAT BAD LOOKING AND YOU'VE ALWAYS WANTED THAT CONVERTIBLE MERCEDES. **T/F**

16 YOU'RE IN AN ESTABLISHED RELATIONSHIP, BUT A DROP DEAD GORGEOUS COLLEAGUE GIVES YOU THE COME ON. YOU'D DUMP YOUR STEADY AND GO FOR GOLD. **T/F**

17 IF A RELATIONSHIP ENDS, YOU'RE BACK ON YOUR FEET AND OUT ON THE PROWL BEFORE YOU CAN EVEN SAY "SINGLE". **T/F**

18 YOUR PAST IS LITTERED WITH EX-LOVERS WHO NOW WON'T GIVE YOU THE TIME OF DAY. **T/F**

19 YOU TEND TO BE THE ONE WHO PUTS THE BOOT IN AND DUMPS A PARTNER BEFORE YOU CAN GET DUMPED. **T/F**

20 YOU'RE THE TYPE TO BLAB TO FRIENDS ABOUT YOUR SEXUAL ENCOUNTERS IN ALL THEIR GORY DETAIL. **T/F**

TURN TO PAGE 88 TO SEE HOW WELL YOU'VE "SCORED".

CHAPTER SIX

CREATIVE AND CHAOTIC OR
LOGICAL AND ORGANISED?

Do you have an organised approach to things, taking the muddle and mess of life and giving it shape and meaning? Always ready with the rational explanation and armed with the ability to push projects through. A doer not a dreamer. Or, do you prefer to stand things on their head, having a penchant for the bizarre, a need to kick against the establishment? Will you rush in where angels fear to tread? To find out, just answer the following questions.

FROM THE FOLLOWING LISTS OF
PERCEIVED STRENGTHS/QUALITIES,
CHOOSE FIVE THAT FIT YOU.

A	B
Tenacious	Resourceful
Accurate	Energetic
Organised	Spontaneous
Logical	Creative
Consistent	Adaptable
Industrious	Enthusiastic
Responsible	Daring
Focused	Curious

Now, FROM THE FOLLOWING LISTS
OF POSSIBLE FAULTS/WEAKNESSES,
PICK FIVE THAT YOU TEND TO FALL INTO
(IF YOU HAVE TROUBLE WITH THIS QUESTION,
NO DOUBT FRIENDS AND FAMILY ON HAND WILL
BE ONLY TOO WILLING TO HELP!).

A	B
Control freak	Careless
Inflexible	Irresponsible
Pedantic	Frivolous
Critical	Inattentive
Cautious	Disorganised
Sarcastic	Superficial
Obsessive	Undisciplined

YOUR WRITTEN WORK TENDS TO LOOK LIKE THIS:

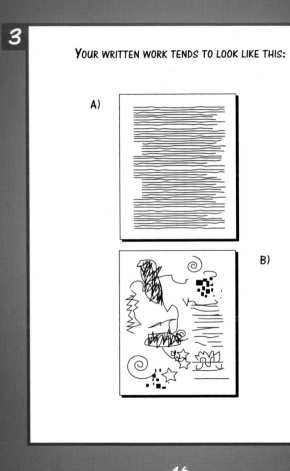

A)

B)

YOU WOULD PREFER TO BE DESCRIBED AS...

A) Perceptive

B) Innovative

THE QUALITY YOU WOULD LOOK FOR IN ANOTHER PERSON IS...

A) Consideration

B) Spontaneity

WHICH OF THESE COLOURS DO YOU PREFER?

A) Purple   B) Blue

7

WHICH REACTION DO YOU RELATE TO WHEN
YOU HEAR THE WORD "RED"?

A) Rage
B) A primary colour

8

WHEN IT COMES TO PUBLIC SPEAKING
OR INTERVIEWS YOU...

A) Make careful and detailed preparation
B) Fly by the seat of your pants and improvise

9

ARE YOU MORE LIKELY TO FORM
AN OPINION AS A RESULT OF...?

A) Reasoned logic
B) Instinct

10

IF YOU WERE TO CHOOSE ONE OF
THE FOLLOWING SYMBOLS AS YOUR
PERSONAL LOGO, WHICH WOULD IT BE?

A) Rodin's thinker   B) Bird in flight

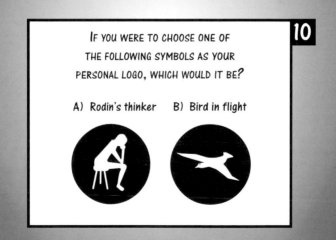

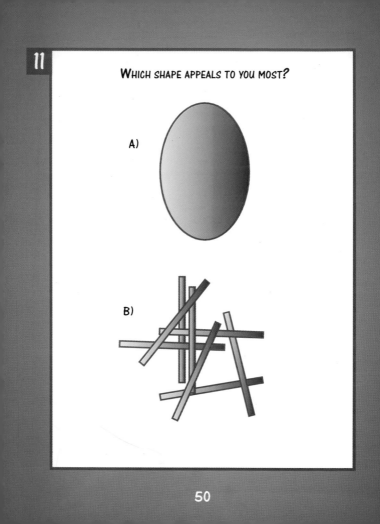

12

DO PEOPLE TEND TO SEE YOU AS...?

A) Someone capable of seeing a project through

B) An ideas person

13

ARE YOU MORE LIKELY TO BE DESCRIBED AS...?

A) A pragmatist

B) A daydreamer

14

ARE YOU MORE OF A...?

A) Team player
B) Opportunist

15

WHICH OF THESE TWO
PICTURES DO YOU PREFER?

A)   B)

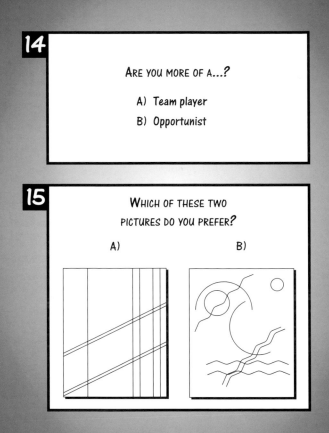

16

WHICH ARE YOU MORE LIKELY TO DO...?

A) Weigh up the odds carefully

B) Take risks

17

ARE YOU DRAWN MORE TO THE...?

A) Traditional

B) Unconventional

18

YOU ARE GOING OUT FOR THE
EVENING AND THE CHOICE IS...

A) An award-winning piece of dramatic theatre

B) A side-splitting stand-up comic

19

WHICH IRRITATES YOU THE MOST?

A) Disorganisation and carelessness

B) Rules and regulations

TURN TO PAGE 89 FOR A QUICK EVALUATION

CHAPTER SEVEN

A SHORT PSYCHOLOGICAL JOURNEY

Let's take a quick stroll round the
psyche. Here is a short journey for
you to take in your mind's eye.
Answer the questions quickly, don't try
to analyse them, just give your initial,
instinctive response. (This is a fun one
to try with a group of friends
after a few drinks!)

YOU GO FOR A WALK AND THE PATH FORKS,
WHICH WAY DO YOU GO?

A) Up over the open plains
B) Down to the wooded valley

YOU COME ACROSS A BEAR.
WHAT TYPE OF BEAR IS IT?

THERE IS A GUN NEARBY.
WHAT TYPE OF GUN IS IT?
DO YOU PICK IT UP?

IF SO, DO YOU WANT TO JUST CARRY
IT FOR SECURITY OR WOULD YOU BE
PREPARED TO USE IT?

You WALK ON A LITTLE FURTHER AND FIND A KEY.
WHAT TYPE OF KEY IS IT?
DESCRIBE IT.

Do you...

A) pick it up or

B) leave it where it is?

YOU THEN FIND A VASE.
WHAT TYPE OF VASE IS IT?
DESCRIBE IT.

AGAIN, DO YOU...

A) pick it up or
B) leave it where it is?

⋮

↓

YOU COME TO SOME WATER.
VISUALISE WHAT FORM THIS WATER TAKES.

⋮

↓

BEYOND THE WATER IS A PARTICULAR
TYPE OF LANDSCAPE.
DESCRIBE WHAT YOU SEE.

FOR AN EXPLANATION AND ANALYSIS, SEE PAGE 90

COLD

BLACK

RAINBOW

GREY

WARM

CHAPTER EIGHT

THE COLOURS OF YOUR MIND

Do you look at the world through
rose-tinted spectacles or do you
paint everything in black and white?
People of similar traits often prefer
certain colours and these are
closely linked to the emotions.
Answer the following questions
to see if you are a colourful
character or a cold fish...

WHITE

HOT

SUBTLE

BRIGHT

COLOUR

1

Do you like...?

A) Strong, bright, vibrant colours
B) Cool, subtle, delicate shades

2

Do you feel more comfortable in...?

A) A sunny, brightly-lit room
B) A cosy, subtly lit room
C) The dark

3

FROM THE COLOUR SAMPLES ILLUSTRATED
OVERLEAF, CHOOSE THE TWO COLOURS YOU
LIKE THE MOST, IN ORDER OF PREFERENCE, AND THEN
THE ONE YOU DISLIKE OR LIKE THE LEAST

A) ....

B) ....

C) ....

4

IF YOU WERE GOING TO DESCRIBE YOURSELF AS ONE OF
THE SAMPLE COLOURS, WHICH WOULD IT BE?

....

5

GET YOUR PARTNER, A CLOSE FRIEND OR A RELATIVE
TO DESCRIBE YOU AS ONE OF THE COLOURS

....

COLOUR PALATTE

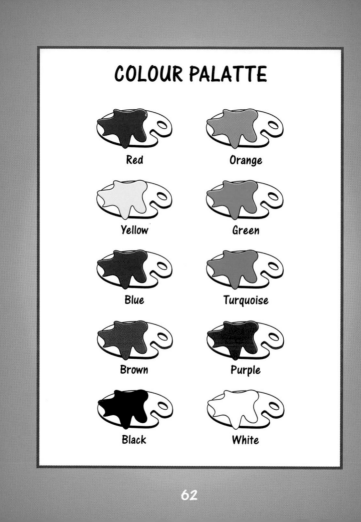

Red

Orange

Yellow

Green

Blue

Turquoise

Brown

Purple

Black

White

6

YOU HAVE A SPECIAL OCCASION COMING UP.
WHICH OF THE COLOURS WOULD YOU CHOOSE
FOR THAT SPECIAL OUTFIT?

....

7

WHICH OF THE COLOURS DO YOU
ACTUALLY WEAR THE MOST?

....

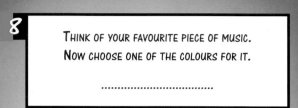

8 | THINK OF YOUR FAVOURITE PIECE OF MUSIC. NOW CHOOSE ONE OF THE COLOURS FOR IT.

....

9 | IF YOU WERE TO CHOOSE YOUR OWN HERALDIC BANNER, WHICH OF THESE COLOURS WOULD YOU CHOOSE?

....

THE SEASONS OF THE YEAR ARE
TRADITIONALLY ASSOCIATED WITH CERTAIN
COLOURS. WHICH SEASON DO YOU PREFER
AND PICK THREE OF THE COLOURS
SUGGESTIVE OF THAT SEASON?

A) Spring ....

B) Summer ....

C) Autumn ....

D) Winter ....

10

QUESTIONS 3-10

ON THE GRAPH BELOW, COLOUR IN ONE SQUARE
FOR EACH POSITIVE ANSWER. FOR THE COLOUR
YOU DISLIKE/LIKE LEAST, PUT A CROSS AND MAKE
A NOTE OF ITS PROPERTIES AS THESE ARE THE
ONES LEAST LIKELY TO APPLY OR APPEAL TO YOU.

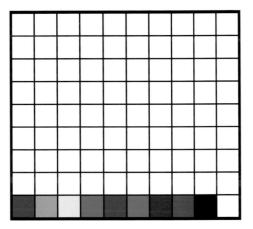

SO, ARE YOU A COLOUR-COORDINATED PERSONALITY OR DO YOU
CLASH VIOLENTLY? TURN TO PAGE 92 TO FIND OUT!

CHAPTER NINE

EROTIC AND HUNGRY FOR LIFE OR FRIGID AND HIGHLY STRUNG?

Some people seem to want to grab a big slice of life and squeeze the last drop out of it, while others are a tad more restrained in their approach. Are you the touchy feely type or strictly hands off? Do you react not so much to cute Cupid as to erotic Eros and do you see the world as one big banquet or a meagre portion of bread and cheese? Answer the following to gauge your appetite ...

1

WOULD ANY OR ALL OF THE FOLLOWING
FEATURE REGULARLY IN YOUR BEDROOM ANTICS?
BABY OIL, ICE CREAM, CHOCOLATE,
YOGHURT, FRUIT ... YOU GET THE PICTURE!

A) You buy in bulk – it saves time.

B) OK, so you have the odd rub-a-dub-dub
midnight feast.

C) Don't be revolting.

2

DO YOU PREFER YOUR PARTNERS
PUNGENT OR PERFUMED?

A) A good whiff of natural body scent.

B) A quick dab of something seductive.

C) Squeaky clean and fresh.

3

SOFT AND SENSITIVE? WHAT DO YOU LIKE
TO SLIP ON NEXT TO YOUR SKIN?

A) Something silky, sensual and saucy.
B) Something clean, cotton and comfortable.
C) Something pristine and practical.
After all, you might get run over by a bus!

4

WE ALL HAVE A PARTICULAR PREFERENCE –
WHETHER IT BE STRONG HANDS, OR SHAPELY FEET.
WHAT GRABS YOUR ATTENTION FIRST?

A) Cute butt, long legs, an impressive chest.
B) Smiling eyes and a warm personality.
C) A fine mind.

5

DO YOU LIKE FOOD THAT YOU CAN REALLY GET TO GRIPS WITH?

A) Mmm yes, there's no other way to eat lobsters, oysters, asparagus...

B) Finger food can be fun – a little messy, but fun.

C) That's precisely why cutlery was invented!

6

A GOOD SOAKING FOR YOU ENTAILS...

A) Sharing a Jacuzzi, hot tub or a roll in the mud with the gang.

B) A warm bubbly bath and having your back scrubbed.

C) Colonic irrigation.

NOW TURN TO PAGE 94 TO
GET A "FEEL" FOR THINGS

CHAPTER TEN

GRAPHOLOGY

For generations, graphology, the art of handwriting analysis, has been used as a method of determining character and personality. Do you cross your t's and dot your i's, or is it just one long scrawl? What does your handwriting reveal about you? For this test, take an unlined piece of paper and write a short paragraph. Make sure you include a sprinkling of capitals, the personal pronoun I, a mixture of short and long words and take care to sign the written text with your usual signature. Examine your handwriting and answer the following questions.

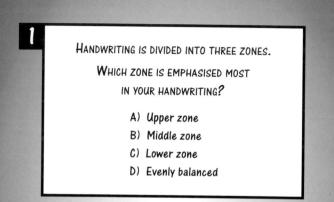

TO WHAT DEGREE DO YOU JOIN LETTERS TOGETHER?

2

A) Medium connection (only 3/4 letters or short words linked)

B) Good connection (letters well joined, some longer words)

C) Extreme connection (whole words, sentences, even lines of writing joined)

D) Disconnected (only 2/3 letters joined or not linked at all)

A) Life is a jest and all things show it
I thought so once, but now I know it.

B) Life is a jest and all things show it
I thought so once, but now I know it

C) Life is a jest and all things show it
I thought so once, but now I know it.

D) Life is a jest and all things show it
I thought so once, but now I know it

WHICH OF THE FOUR MAIN KINDS OF WRITING CONNECTION IS TYPICAL OF YOUR STYLE?

A) Arcade (curved clockwise)

B) Angular

C) Garland (curved anti-clockwise)

D) Thread

_____

THE COPY-BOOK SIZE FOR HANDWRITING IS APPROXIMATELY 9MM. IS YOUR WRITING...?

A) Large (over 10mm)

B) Small (under 8mm)

C) Medium (approx. 9mm)

A) *tomorrow*

B) *tomorrow*

C) *tomorrow*

5

IN WHICH DIRECTION DOES YOUR WRITING TEND TO LEAN?

- A) Left tendencies
- B) Upright
- C) Right tendencies
- D) Mixed

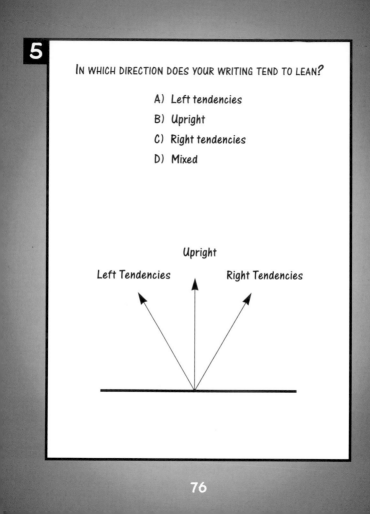

IS YOUR WRITING...?

A) Regular (size, width, slant all fairly constant)

B) Irregular (complete lack of uniformity)

A) the moving finger writes, and having writ
moves on : nor all thy piety nor wit
shall lure it back to cancel half a line,
nor all thy tears wash out a word of it.

B) the moving finger writes, and having writ
moves on: nor all thy piety nor wit
Should lure it back to cancel half a line,
Nor all thy tears wash out a word of it.

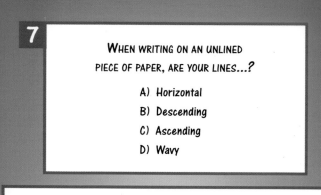

7

WHEN WRITING ON AN UNLINED PIECE OF PAPER, ARE YOUR LINES...?

A) Horizontal
B) Descending
C) Ascending
D) Wavy

A) The wheel has come full circle

B) The wheel has come full circle

C) The wheel has come full circle

D) The wheel has come full circle

DO YOUR LETTERS SHOW...?

A) Simplification

B) Flourishes and ornamentation

C) Neglect (parts of letters are indistinct or missing)

A) Twisting and turning, spiralling down Towards their destined meeting ground.

B) Twisting and turning, Spiralling down Towards their destined meeting ground.

C) Twisting & turning, spiralling down Towards their destined meeting ground.

9

Is your writing...?

A) Quite easy to read
B) Quite difficult to read
C) Almost illegible

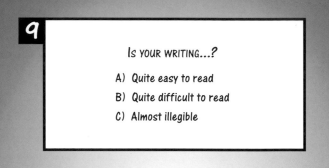

A) The night is long that never finds the day.

B) The night is long that never finds the day

C) The night is long that never finds the day

10

IN RELATION TO THE REST OF THE TEXT, ARE YOUR
CAPITALS AND THE PERSONAL PRONOUN I...?

- A) Average size
- B) Smaller
- C) Larger
- D) Very large

11

HOW HAVE YOU SIGNED YOUR NAME?

- A) Same size as text
- B) Smaller than text
- C) Larger than text

AND IS THE SLANT...?

- D) Same as text
- E) Different to text

WHERE HAVE YOU PLACED YOUR SIGNATURE IN RELATION TO THE TEXT?

A) To the right of the text
B) In the centre
C) To the left of the text

A)
Best wishes

Lisa Thurlow

B)
Kind regards

George Morden

C)
 yours faithfully

Helen Brooke

TURN TO PAGE 95 FOR YOUR WRITTEN ANALYSIS

CHAPTER ONE

SCORING THE QUESTIONNAIRE

To find out which type you are, add up all the numbers you have circled to reach your overall score.

SCORE 81-100
Road rage, trolley rage, world rage. You see life as one big battle – conquer and control is your motto. Take it easy, take the weight off your blood pressure. You're like an unexploded firework: ready to go off and burn out.

SCORE 61-80
Competitive, ambitious, controlling, impatient, irritable, rushed. Sound familiar? You exhibit classic characteristics and are positively addicted to stress. Time to take that course in relaxation...

SCORE 41-60
You are well-motivated and moderately ambitious but are not dominated by work. You react to the stresses and strains of everyday life in a measured way, but are quite capable of getting the bit between your teeth when necessary.

SCORE 31-40
You show typical calm characteristics: casual, easy-going, patient and unambitious. You take life as it comes and in your stride, but a little passion and fire on occasions wouldn't go amiss.

SCORE 20-30
A single cell amoeba has more ambition and drive. You're so laid back you're almost horizontal.

CHAPTER TWO

SCORING AND EVALUATION

A) answers score 5
B) answers score 3
C) answers score 1

TOTAL YOUR SCORE AND READ THE CATEGORY INTO WHICH YOU FALL...

56-70

You are a professional romantic. You seem to be in love with the idea of being in love. The question is, does it matter who is on the receiving end so long as you can play the romantic lead? Either that or you have genuinely been reduced to mush by someone special.

31-55

You like to put up a world weary front from time to time, but, like most people, you want to ride off into the sunset with the one you love. Peel a few layers and you are all soft and squidgy underneath.

14-30

Oh dear! Oh dear! You have hardly a romantic bone in your body. A high priest of pragmatism and practicality, you have no time for soppy sentiment.

CHAPTER THREE

EXPLANATION:

Expressions such as "a wolf in sheep's clothing", "a real snake in the grass", and "free as a bird" are commonplace. We frequently apply animal imagery to others and to ourselves, and this is what this exercise has been about: image.

● Your first choice is how you would like to be seen, your ideal image.
● Your second choice is how you think others see you, the image you project.
● Your third choice is how you see yourself, how you think you really are.
● Your own choices should tell you a lot about yourself, but, just in case, let's spell it out. For each or all of the animals selected, did you choose mainly:

A QUALITIES:

You beast you! You want to be seen as mad, bad and dangerous to know.

B QUALITIES:

Certainly no problem with self-image here, you're positively oozing animal magnetism – or at least you think you are!

C QUALITIES:

Regular feeding, lots of exercise, having your tummy tickled on occasion and you see yourself as a steadfast friend for life.

D QUALITIES

Do you ever come out of your hole? Your self-image is virtually non-existent. You are either going on the endangered species list or into mythology along with Nessie and Bigfoot.

CHAPTER FOUR

Each answer has certain letters entered against it.
Circle your answer. Then, when you have checked all
the answers, count up the number of times
a letter occurs as a result of your choice.
Enter the total for that letter on the score card.

	A)	B)	C)	D)	E)	F)	G)
1	X, O, E	I, P, A	W, T, E	D, R, O	R, E, D		
shape 2	E	R	X	T	A	I, A	
colour 2	E, O	T, S	P	T, P	E, W		
3	E, X	R	W	S, U	O, D	I	D, R
4	P	S, T	E, X	A, R			
5	P	E, X	A, W	S, T			
6	T	P	E	W			
7	W	U, I	X				
8	W, X	T, I					
9	W	D, E	T, I	E, W			
10	T	P					
11	O	W	U, R				
12	X, D	P	R, E	A, W			
13	W	E	P	X, O			

A	D	E	I	O	P	R	S	T	U	W	X

SCORE CARD:

EACH LETTER CORRESPONDS TO A PARTICULAR GROUP OF PERSONALITY TRAITS, AS LISTED BELOW. ARE YOU WELL-BALANCED AND WELL-ROUNDED OR DO YOU NEED TO SHAVE A FEW CORNERS OFF THOSE EDGES, OR, HAVE THINGS GONE COMPLETELY PEAR-SHAPED?

CHARACTER KEY

X = Extrovert, egotist, enthusiastic, engaging

I = Introvert, reserved, logical, self-controlled

W = Warm, balanced, adaptable, generous, nurturing

R = Restless, moody, inquisitive, changeable

S = Sensitive, self-conscious, spiritual

E = Energetic, physical, passionate

A = Artistic, creative, communicative, expressive

P = Practical, steady, down-to-earth, reliable

D = Dynamic, driven, ambitious, aggressive

O = Obstinate, wilful, stubborn, intractable

T = Thoughtful, tactful, passive, careful

U = Unreliable, easily influenced, lacking self-esteem

CHAPTER FIVE

EVALUATION

MOST STATEMENTS WERE "TRUE"

Talk about love them and leave them! Commitment really is a dirty word as far as you're concerned. Even on a "one night stand" you probably don't stay the night. You are either callous, cruel and calculating or frightened to death of getting hurt.

A MIX OF "TRUE" AND "FALSE"

Well, you're no saint, but not exactly a sinner either. You are happy to "play the game of love" and "play the field" at times, but, if the right relationship comes along, you'll try your best to make it work.

MOST STATEMENTS WERE "FALSE"

What are you – some kind of emotional doormat? A sacrificial victim on the altar of love? Go on a self-assertive course. Find the odd erogenous zone. Just get a grip!

CHAPTER SIX

SCORING AND EVALUATION

Count up how many A characteristics you logged up in questions 1 and 2 and how many times you went for A) as your answer in questions 3-19. Now do the same for the Bs.

MAINLY As

Your middle name is Mr Spock. You're logical, accurate, thoughtful, organised, industrious, responsible and tenacious. You have great powers of concentration. You're disciplined and patient. You are also quite capable of going it alone and sticking to your principles even if all around you are wavering. However, you do like to have things clear cut and, when taken to extremes, this can become narrow-mindedness. Other weaknesses could include an obsessive attention to detail that means you fail to see the bigger picture and a tendency to pessimism.

MAINLY Bs

You like to find the unconventional way of doing things and to experiment..You're a risk taker who loves to wheel and deal. Free-spirited and versatile, you can be innovative and visionary. However, you should be careful this doesn't slip into irresponsibility. A rebel without a cause who just likes to take a poke at tradition for the sake of it. Your impulsive nature can be appealing, but could also get you into trouble!

CHAPTER SEVEN

EXPLANATION AND ANALYSIS

Option A) the open plain indicates a willingness to expose yourself to risks, that you are open to new ideas and experiences.

Option B) the wooded valley suggests a greater need for a more sheltered environment, shaded and protected.

The bear indicates your relationships with other people, whether you see them as threatening (a great big grizzly) or a pushover (a cute teddy bear).

The gun reflects how you deal with other people – fully armed with a double-barrelled shotgun or unarmed and completely defenceless. Perhaps only a small pistol up your sleeve – just in case!

For men, the key indicates how they see their own sexuality (little chubb lock or great big rusty old thing). And whether they pick it up or not relates to their self-esteem and how comfortable they are with that image.

For women, the key relates to their ideal of male sexuality (good solid housekey or something that's going to open Pandora's box). Whether they pick it up or not again shows how comfortable they are with that image.

With the vase, the gender applications are reversed. So, girls, is it a graceful Grecian urn, priceless Ming vase or a cracked bit of earthenware with some daffodils stuck inside? Let's just draw a veil over what the men have been visualising.

Again, is the vase left behind or safely tucked away and treasured?

The water imagery is how you see your immediate way ahead. A cool refreshing stream, raging rapids or muddy pond?

Finally, the landscape of the future awaits. Do you see it as a land of milk and honey, a barren wasteland, or do you still have some mountains to climb?

Hopefully this little exercise has given you some clues as to your current state of mind.

CHAPTER EIGHT

COLOUR COMMENTARY

1.   A) This choice indicates an extrovert personality, one that is drawn to the outer world. B) Decidedly cooler, calmer, more introverted, drawn to the inner world.

2.   A) Indicates a more physically active type B) Indicates a more thoughtful, sedentary type C) You're a mole.

The colour graph on page 66 should show you your colour preferences and whether any colours are particularly dominant.

COLOUR/CHARACTER ASSOCIATIONS:

An even spread of colours: a real rainbow personality. You are either a very balanced, harmonious individual or a chameleon-like character who wants to blend in and change yourself at will.

RED: – Quite the emotional powerhouse: temperamental, outgoing, assertive, impulsive, sexually active, competitive – but this could all be a flashy bluff for certain insecurities. Someone overly attracted to red often shows a lack of emotional control. A real dislike of red is unusual, possibly indicating frustration and thwarted ambition, a need to retreat from social contact.

ORANGE: – This is one for the party animal: informal, enjoys physical enjoyment and comfort, sociable, a happy extrovert; but orange can clash violently, so you're either an individualist or you haven't any dress sense. Orange can also be seen as frivolous – you might not be taken seriously!

YELLOW: – Yellows are direct, confident, optimistic, self-sufficient and very disciplined with high energy levels. They need to be in control, are frequently attention seeking and talkative. A favourite colour of children, perhaps you can be a little infantile at times.

GREEN: – Flexible, relaxed, natural and trusting. Greens are well adjusted, balanced, harmonious and neat. However, green can be an indication of a cautious or escapist nature and, of course, it is traditionally associated with envy, disease or unlucky superstitions.

BLUE: – True blue all the way! Calm, accommodating, reserved, self-doubting, reliable and dependable. Blue is associated with thoughtful introspection, possibly a tad smug and definitely not radical. However blues can be seen as cold, anxious, and slightly melancholic.

TURQUOISE: – Something of an enigmatic colour with a sense of its own worth. An individual choice showing a sense of balance, but can indicate fastidiousness. A little picky are we?

PURPLE: – An indication of a restless character, socially bold, conceptual, radical, undisciplined, and suspicious. It is something of a showy colour indicating a love of display, being a bit over-the-top, outrageous or pompous.

BROWN: – One for the earthy individual more attracted to home comforts. Practical, respectable, restrained, down-to-earth, if a little boring and predictable – a hint here of the need for fulfilment.

BLACK: – Often associated with danger and romance, black has an air of sophistication, rejection of authority, excitement, style and sex – a very self-conscious colour choice. Yet it is in fact a very safe colour that won't really stand out. It can put up barriers, seem menacing, negative, spiritually depressing, not always the colour of someone who feels confident and in control.

WHITE: – Uncompromising, demanding, aspirational, white is often linked with purity and spirituality, and, conversely, luxury, but it lacks emotional warmth. It can seem cold and sterile – a bit holier than thou in attitude.

CHAPTER NINE

SCORING AND EVALUATION

A) answers score 10
B) answers score 5
C) answers score 1

TOTAL YOUR SCORE AND READ THE
CATEGORY INTO WHICH YOU FALL...

50-60

Wow! You make your average hedonist seem fairly straight-laced. Life's just one great orgy of the senses as far as you're concerned. Remember, over-indulgence can make you sick.

12-49

You know how to let your hair down and have a good time. The odd bit of gratuitous sensual gratification doesn't go amiss, but you also know when enough's enough.

6-11

You are probably thinking of opening up your own sensory deprivation centre – either that or you are completely tuned into the spiritual and abstract rather than the physical.

CHAPTER TEN

EACH ANSWER SCORES A CERTAIN LETTER.
CIRCLE YOUR ANSWER AND WHEN YOU HAVE FINISHED GOING
THROUGH YOUR ANSWERS, COUNT UP HOW MANY TIMES
YOU HAVE SCORED EACH PARTICULAR LETTER.

1. The Three Zones	A) A	B) N	C) P	D) H	
2. Connected/Disconnected	A) H	B) I	C) A	D) S	
3. Form of Connection	A) I	B) E	C) H	D) M	
4. Size	A) E	B) S	C) H		
5. Slant	A) I	B) S	C) E	D) M	
6. Regularity	A) H	B) M			
7. Direction of Lines	A) N	B) I	C) E	D) M	
8. Letter Formation	A) S	B) E	C) M		
9. Legibility	A) H	B) S	C) M		
10. Capitals and the Personal Pronoun I	A) H	B) I	C) S	D) E	
11. Signature	A) H	B) I	C) E		
	and	D) N	E) M		
12. Placement of signature	A) E	B) N	C) I		

95

Look at the key below and read the text next to the letters which appeared most in your scores to see which characteristics are revealed in your writing.

KEY:

A – Abstract: idealism, aspiration, meditation, imagination and intellectual pursuits, may lack practicality, a dreamer.

E – Extrovert: vitality, spontaneity, ambition, forward looking and outward looking, can be impatient, compulsive and egotistical.

H – Harmonious: well-adjusted, an all-rounder, common-sense, good self-esteem, balance between mental and practical application, compassionate and adaptable.

I – Introvert: reserved, inward looking, rational, formal, sensitive, shy, concerned with the past and the inner self, in extreme cases can become depressive.

M – Moody: mixed emotions, creative, changeable, emotional, can be capricious or unsure, reflecting the possibility of inner conflict and unhappiness.

N – Natural: sociable, pragmatic, reliable, steadfast, concerned with the here and now, sometimes a little too predictable.

P – Physical: sexual, practical, instinctive, material, and, unless well balanced with other qualities, tending to self-interest.

S – Self-sufficient: independent, clear-headed, logical, modest, objective, can appear cold and a little dry.